Number One ·

Be curious, inves
and feel good

Name:

....

If lost, please return to:

....

....

....

Thanks for caring!

Who are the Canal & River Trust?

Manchester Ship Canal cost £15 million to construct – in today's money that would be around £1.65 billion. It is still used today to transport goods.

We are a charity, here to protect over 2,000 miles of waterways in England and Wales. We're custodians of a rich, living history but we look forward to a brighter, better future too.

We love and care for your canals and rivers, because everyone deserves a place to escape, whether it's on the water; on foot; on a bike; with friends or on your own. Take a fresh look at what's happening on your waterway. It's closer than you think.

As a charity, we rely on our supporters and a passionate team of staff and volunteers. We work together to create better, more open spaces, breathing new life into our canals and rivers. That means joining forces with the communities that live and work around our waterways.

Canals and rivers offer inspiring ways to bring learning to life. The Canal & River Trust delivers a range of highly-regarded learning programmes designed to inspire and enthuse young people about our wonderful waterways.

Working with schools and uniformed groups, the Trust's education team aims to inspire children's learning by connecting them to canals and rivers. Our education programmes are highly regarded by teachers and group leaders, largely due to the support of experienced education volunteers, who lead enjoyable and inspiring visits on the towpath, in your classroom or at one of our museums.

Our exciting new STEM (Science, Technology, Engineering and Maths) learning programme is targeted at secondary schools and aims to inspire young people about STEM careers available along our waterways. Developed in partnership with graduates from the Rolls Royce Graduate Scheme, our STEM programme offers free workshops to key stage three students. From the hydraulics of boat lifts to the erosion of river banks, STEM along our waterways is limitless.

The Canal & River Trust's waterways, museums and attractions offer a fantastic opportunity to improve our health and wellbeing. This journal is designed to take you on a fun-filled journey. You'll discover and explore the amazing 250-year old history of our waterways, and the rich environment they support today, as well as learning how to be active and feel good, and de-stress when things get tough.

I invite you to experience the wonders and enjoy the benefits of our beautiful, inspiring waterways.

Richard Parry, CEO of the Canal & River Trust

Contents:

Part 1   **Visiting us**

Helpful hints on how to use this book, activities you can do during your waterways and museum visits.

Part 2   **Reflections**

Activities to use on your return home or back to school. These help deepen your understanding of the waterways and its people, reflect on your experience and help you plan for your next visit.

Part 3   **Journaling**

Moving on from the waterways experience, this part focuses on you as a person, providing a wellbeing journal and pathway for you to build on what you're good at, and your skills to cope with difficult times. It concentrates on your personal development, and how you can flourish.

Part 4   **Useful information**

Guidance and information for teachers, parents, guardians and group leaders on the education approach and underlying methodology.

Part 5   **Acknowledgements**

Information on the writers, publisher and illustrators and the people, schools and organisations that have helped and supported the development of Number One.

Did you know, at a steady walking pace, a horse can tow up to 50 times its own weight?

Welcome

Welcome to Number One. This journal is designed to help you learn more about yourself through visiting our canals and rivers. You will discover their fascinating past, present and future while also learning what you do well; growing in self-confidence and finding out how to 'bounce back' when things are tough.

We hope you find it an enjoyable and fun experience, and one where you'll notice the difference in yourselves.

Tim Slack, Appreciating People and Helen Evans, Canal & River Trust

You'll find some questions to reflect on wherever you see this compass symbol...

From your visit to the canals and/or the National Waterways Museums, write down your answers to these questions:

• What was the best thing you saw on your visit?

....

....

• What did you enjoy doing most?

....

....

• What was the most interesting thing you learned about?

....

....

Part 1.

Visiting the waterways & museums

A winding hole is a widened area of the canal used for turning boats around. Before boats had engines, the wind was used to assist with turning.

Be active and keep learning!

Discover canal and river people and places, both now and in the past, using the activities in this section. You can do these anywhere in the country, but do try to visit one of our museums or visitor attractions if you have one nearby.

Do these activities in any order. Find the ones you like most first and then try the more difficult ones (some will need a bit of research). Get people to help you and have fun!

Get creative

You'll have noticed that many of the boats and their equipment have colourful designs – often of fantasy castles and roses. The art form is called 'Roses & Castles', and is part of folk art traditions common in many cultures.

This activity is in three parts:

1.) Firstly, research the colours and designs used, and what they represent*

2.) Complete the Roses & Castles design

3.) Finally, research the designs used for canal boat names, then create and draw your own boat name.

*To find examples of the colours used in the Roses & Castles art, look at the boats on the waterways or research online.

An aqueduct carries a canal over something such as a road, valley, river or railway

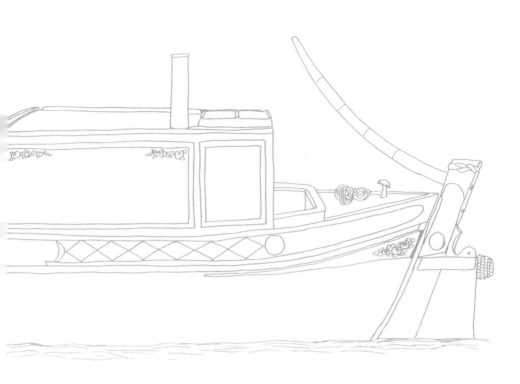

• What did you enjoy about the activity?

....

....

• When you finished completing the activity, what did you notice in yourself? Did you feel relaxed?

....

....

• If you did it again, how would you make it even better?

....

....

Did you know our canals and rivers get invaded by aliens? The American Crayfish and Japanese Knotweed are two of the worst alien invaders for our native British wildlife

Mindfulness Zone

Canal & River Trust

Take notice

Mindfulness is simply noticing. How do you feel? What can you see, smell, hear, and taste? What is your mind doing and what is happening around you?

Let's find out what happens when you start to take notice.

1.) Find a place near a canal or river where you feel comfortable and won't be disturbed. Take the mindfulness plaque with you or design your own.

2.) Sit down quietly, placing your feet on the floor, with your arms either by your side or in your lap.

3.) Breathe in and out slowly, calming yourself down and feeling your feet connect to the ground. (You can close your eyes if you want to)

4.) Listen. How many different sounds can you hear? Can you identify them all?

5.) Notice. How do you feel?

Spend a few minutes doing this activity. Practice until you can do this for five minutes or more. If you enjoy it, why not set up a mindfulness zone at home or at school? (You can find more information about mindfulness on page **92**.)

Let yourself relax. The first time you do this, try doing it for two minutes, then build up to three, four and five minutes in the future.

Now consider these two questions...

• What did you like about it?

....

....

• How do you think this can help other people, and what could it do?

....

....

• How did it help you?

....

....

Houses and homes

See if you can spot the difference between the four kitchens on the next page, from the National Waterways Museum at Ellesmere Port. Can you put them in order from the oldest to the most modern? When you've had a good look, answer these questions...

How do these kitchens compare to your own?

....

....

....

....

What is the same and what does your kitchen have that none of these do?

....

....

....

....

What is a starvationer?

Investigate!

How long is a canal boat? Investigate this question using pacing.

Walk normally along the length of the boat or lock. Each step is approximately 30cm. Use this information to estimate the length. If there's a bridge over the lock, you could use the same method to estimate the width, and use these measurements to work out the area of the lock. (Area = length x width)

Did you know? Boaters had to 'leg' through most tunnels using their feet to propel them along. This was because many narrow tunnels had no towpath running through them.

Watch a boat at a lock flight

Time how long it takes to go through the first lock, then estimate how long it will take to complete the flight... Keep your timer running and see if your estimate was correct; this might require some practise! Try both narrow and broad beam locks. A narrow lock can only take one narrow boat, while a broad beam can fit two in, side by side. Broad beam locks can also take single boats that are wider than 10ft.

• **Which animals love to live in and around waterways?**

....

....

• Can you identify a food chain from the plants and animals around you?

....

....

• Take a look at our Canal and River Habitats pack to find out more about food chains. You'll find it online at: www.canalrivertrust.org.uk/explorers

....

....

Wildlife surveys

What makes a hedge? Measure a length of hedge. Count and identify the plants in each metre.

A good way to investigate this question is to carry out a 'minibeast hunt'.

A quadrat is a small area of habitat, usually one square metre in size. Mark out a quadrat, using string to mark out a square metre on the ground and pegs to hold it in place. Collect and identify the minibeasts in your quadrat (a 'minibeast' is simply a small animal – spiders, snails, slugs, beetles, centipedes, worms, earwigs and caterpillars are just a few examples). Compare what you find here to a quadrat in a different place.

• Which of the activities did you enjoy the most, and why?

....

....

• What surprised you in doing these activities?

....

....

• Which activity would you like to do more of and why?

....

....

From the towpath

Getting out and about on the towpath helps you feel good, have fun and be healthy. Try these towpath activities and see if you can improve your wellbeing (you'll find more information on wellbeing on page 90).

1. How many of these structures can you spot while walking, running, cycling or fishing from the towpath?

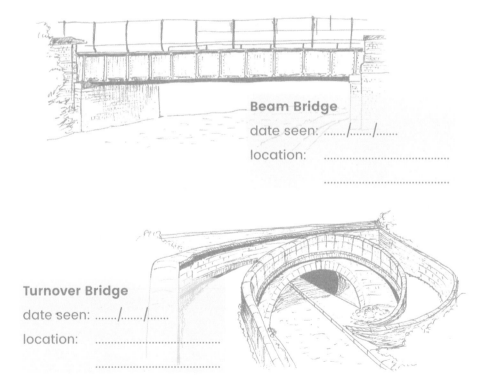

Beam Bridge

date seen: ..../......./.......

location: ....

....

Turnover Bridge

date seen: ..../......./.......

location: ....

....

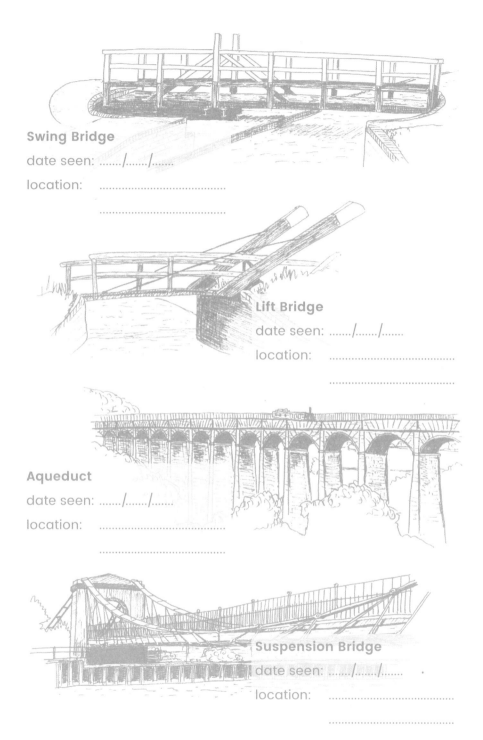

Swing Bridge

date seen: ..../......./.......

location: ....

....

Lift Bridge

date seen: ..../......./.......

location: ....

....

Aqueduct

date seen: ..../......./.......

location: ....

....

Suspension Bridge

date seen: ..../......./.......

location: ....

....

2. Walk the canal towpath and collect things like twigs, leaves, mosses and bird feathers. Using glue and paper, create your own piece of natural art.

3. Go on a towpath walk and create a journey stick as you go along. Journey sticks have been used for hundreds of years by many people around the globe. They can retell a story about a journey, or help you retrace your steps using the items you've collected. You could use things like feathers, leaves and twigs you've found along the way, and tie them to your stick. Historically, landmarks and waymarkers would have been carved into the stick, but we're pretty sure you'll find it easier to tie yours on with some string! You'll find plenty more information online if you need it...

4. Walk 1,000 steps along a canal or river. How many interesting things can you spot?

5. Sit and sketch...

6. Find a plant or animal that you don't recognise. Can you make up a name for it, based on the way it looks and behaves?

7. Think about the Be an author task on page 42. Try one...

Use the blank pages at the back of this book.

Bingley 5 Rise

• Which activities did you enjoy most?

....

....

• What was the most challenging, and why?

....

....

• Which activity helped you understand about the importance of the waterways and why?

....

....

Ask a volunteer

Volunteering is an important part of being a good citizen and supports your health and wellbeing. Canal & River Trust has hundreds of volunteers who work along our waterways, in our museums and visitor attractions and in schools.

Can you find one to interview? They are very friendly! Here are some questions you could ask them:

1. What is your role as a volunteer and what do you do?
2. Why is volunteering important to you?
3. What skills and knowledge do you bring to the role?
4. What do you like about the role?
5. Can you tell us a story about when your volunteering has helped people and/or supported the canals?
6. What are the challenges of being a volunteer?
7. How does volunteering help you?

Take a notebook to record the answer.

• What did you enjoy about this activity?

....

....

• What did you learn about volunteering?

....

....

• How could you volunteer and what would you like to do?

....

....

Where's George?

Can you find out where George is today? Here are some clues!

George was built in 1910 as a Leeds & Liverpool Canal short boat. She was designed specifically to fit through the short locks. George carried coal on the Leeds & Liverpool Canal her whole working life. She was reconstructed by National Waterways Museum Ellesmere Port and is now used as a floating outdoor classroom.

• How do you find out where George is?

....

....

• Where does George go in the winter?

....

....

• If you've visited her, what did you do and what did you enjoy about your visit?

....

....

Life afloat

As you'll see from your museum visits, there's lots of information about the lives of the people who lived and worked on the canals. It was a hard life and children were expected to work on the boats from a young age. The day in the life of a boat child, is taken from the National Waterways Archive held at the National Waterways Museum, Ellesmere Port.

How does your life compare to the life of Ethel Parkes?

Day in the life of a boat child:

Information taken from **Waterways Journal, Volume 17: The Story of Charlotte Ethel Parkes.**

A diary of Ethel's day:

wake-up time	When it's light! 5am in the summer
morning	Breakfast (a cup of tea with a spoonful of whisky in to warm up). Feed, groom and harness the horse. Get the boat moving.
afternoon	Steering the boat, usually standing on a stool to see properly! In the winter it gets dark early, so I have to sing or talk so my parents know I am here and safe. Sometimes I walk with the horse over tunnels and through the locks.
evening	Eat dinner on the move or have a short stop to eat. Stable the horse when we arrive. Fetch hot water from the mill to clean the boat.
bed time	a quick wash and bed. We go to sleep when all the jobs are finished.

Create a diary of your day. What would Ethel think of it?

wake-up time	
morning	
afternoon	
evening	
bed time	

• What do you think this young person living on the canal needs to be good at?

....

....

• Looking at how tough their lives were, what things do you do well and how do you bounce back when things get difficult?

....

....

• What are the biggest differences between your lives?

....

....

Be an engineer

Can you build a narrow boat cabin at home or in your classroom?
You will need...

- a clear wall and floor space
- masking tape
- art and craft materials
  (paper, scissors, measuring tape and pens)
- rope, poles and stands
  (or a couple of chairs, if you want to do the den version)
- permission to use masking tape on the walls and floor

Mark out the width, height and length of the cabin with masking
tape on your clear wall and floor space. To add the feeling of roof
and walls use ropes, poles and sheets, or a couple of chairs with
the sheet draped over. (If you use poles, you'll need to work out
how to get them to stand up...)

width = 2 metres; length = 2.5 metres; height = 1.5 metres

Do some research to find out what the inside of the cabin
would look like. Use the boat cabin images for advice. Can you
reconstruct the inside of the cabin? How many people can you fit
inside your cabin? Could you live in this space with your family?

Helpful hints

• Use your arts and crafts materials to fill in spaces for the bed/seating, fold down table and storage. You will find even less space available for crew!

• If you visit one of the waterways museums you can measure the items in the cabin, then recreate them using paper cut-outs.

• Having built your boat cabin, how many people you can fit in?

....

....

• How tough would it be to live and sleep in this space and could you do it?

....

....

• What do you admire about these canal people?

....

....

Let's eat!

A boat cabin had very little storage and no fridge. This meant food for boat families had to be bought or caught as they travelled. Here are some favourite recipes for boaters.

Navvy's stew:

- 1kg best end of neck of lamb
- seasoned flour
- 2 medium onions
- 4 medium carrots
- parsley
- 1/4 teaspoon English mustard
- fresh thyme
- 1/8 – 1/4 litre Guinness
- 1/4 litre vegetable stock
- oil
- salt and pepper

Winkwell watercress soup:

- 2 bunches fresh watercress
- 0.5kgs potatoes
- 2 large onions
- 1 litre vegetable stock
- 30g butter
- 1 bay leaf
- salt and pepper
- 3-4 tablespoons milk

- Which of these recipes would you like to try?
- Why not have a go at making one yourself and get a real taste of life afloat?

My food diary

Fill in an example of your typical day of meals and snacks, either on a normal school day or on a canal boat holiday.

breakfast
snacks
lunch
snacks
dinner
snacks

• What did you think of the boat food and recipes?

....

....

• What was different to your normal food?

....

....

• Which is the healthier diet, yours or a boater's? Why?

....

....

Challenge yourself

Here are some different types of canal and river boats. They all have a special name. Can you find out their names and spot them out on the waterways? You will also see some of these in our museums.

name: ....

location: ....

....

name: ....

location: ....

....

Did you know, the first
locks were built in the
10th century

name: ....

location: ....

....

name: ....

location: ....

....

Helpful hint

Go to the library or look online. Waterways museums and
waterways magazines are helpful places to start. Why not mark
and name the place where you saw the boat?

name: ....

location: ....

....

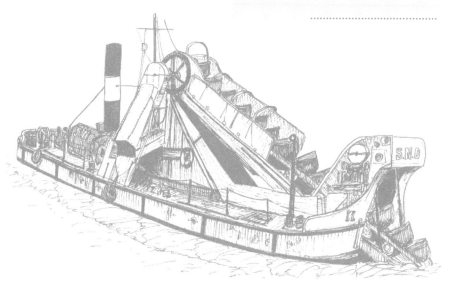

name: ....

location: ....

....

What are navvies?

• What did you enjoy about researching and finding things out?

....

....

• What surprised you?

....

....

• Which are your favourite boats and why?

....

....

Part 2.

Reflections

Did you know? The Tardebigge Flight is the longest set of locks on the canal system! It includes 30 locks in just two and a quarter miles, on the Birmingham & Worcester Canal.

38

Now you've finished your visit to the museum, enjoyed your boat trip, come to the end of your canal boat holiday or made your waterways visit; take some time to think about your experiences.

The activities in this section can be done as a class, uniformed group, as a family, youth group or home education group. They can also be done on your own.

Reflect on your experience

Discuss these questions in small groups, and then try the activity as a big group...

1) Ask each person to tell a story or share an experience of the visit to the museum or the waterways. What were the best bits; what made you nervous and what excited you?

2) What did you enjoy and like about the visit or experience?

3) What did you learn, and what stuck with you the most?

4) What did you notice was different in your life from the lives of the canal people you came across?

5) Imagine you're living on a boat. What would it be like for you and what would you miss from your life now?

Note

Write up your answers on a flipchart. You could create a storybook from the stories.

Group activity

Using a large piece of paper, create the group answers to these questions. Have a discussion first, and make sure everyone in your group agrees...

1) Discuss and list what you enjoyed about the visit. If there are similar reasons add ticks for the number of people.

2) Discuss and list the top seven things you learned through the process.

3) Discuss and list the things you all noticed when comparing how you lived and the canal people.

Personal reflection

After you've completed your group conversation and tasks, write in your book what you liked about the activity. Note down the one most important thing you learned about the waterways or their people. (Note for teachers and group leaders: you could also do this as a group exercise)

Be an author

This creative writing task can be undertaken as a solo or group activity. The helpful hints will support you through the creative writing process.

Visual images

Using a visual image as a prompt is a really effective technique to help you get your initial ideas together. Try to take photographs of the things that strike you as most interesting or unusual, or you could use the pictures in the Trust guide. Make notes on the pictures by zooming in on objects in the scene and labelling them with descriptive phrases. Here's a step by step guide to building the words around the image:

1. Start with what you see and label it with simple nouns, eg barge, river, leaves

2. Think about the colour, shape, size and texture. What would it feel like? Add simple adjectives (describing words). Try some synonyms (words that mean the same thing) or think of adjectives that start with the same letter or sound, like light leaves. That's called alliteration.

3. Now think about movement. If this was in motion, how would it move? What verbs would you use? Try alliteration again. 'Light leaves lift in the gentle summer breeze' has a lovely sound to it, doesn't it?

4. Lastly, to add even more descriptive detail, describe how the object is moving by adding adverbs (words that describe the verb). Let's take the leaves one last time: light leaves lift lazily in the gentle breeze.

Use your senses

Sights, textures and even smells are the perfect place to start, but the real key to creating a vivid description of the scene is to bring the sounds to life. So many of you will have a device with you (your phone, or a tablet) which can be used to record the wonderful sounds of nature. Just as you did with the image, jot down nouns and adjectives, verbs and adverbs which carefully reflect what you could hear. Particular techniques that work well are:

- Onomatopoeia: when the word recreates the sound, eg. whisper, crackle, heave.
- Assonance: when words in sequence share the same middle sound, eg. the barge creaked and heaved in the building breeze.

Making it flow

Once you've got a bank of phrases (a river bank if you've had a particularly creative spell!), you need to put them together in a way that flows. Here's a quick guide to structuring your writing:

• Start with an 'aerial shot' taking in the whole scene. Reveal the time of day (dawn, morning, dusk) and the time of year. Don't TELL your reader, SHOW them: for example, if it's winter, start by describing the sky: 'Under an ice blue sky the canal cracks, its surface solid with cold...'

• Zoom in on your key image. Try one sentence which describes the size and colour, followed by another that describes the texture. Is it moving? Use those brilliant verb phrases you created and make the object move across the scene: 'Gently pushing through the steel grey waters, the barge creaked and heaved in the brisk winter breeze...'

• Choose another object, linked to the first by an action; for example the barge could have approached a lock. Zoom in close. Remember the sound effects. What could you hear? 'The river gushed and gurgled as the lock gates groaned open' paints a really vivid image.

• When you've described everything you want to, zoom out again, back to the aerial shot. Imagine your camera is moving away like at the end of an epic movie. The barge has passed and all is still again. An easy trick is to recycle what you've already written. End with your opening line: 'Once more the canal was still, its surface solid with cold under an ice blue sky.'

This creative writing task has been designed by staff at the Studio School Liverpool, Northern Schools Trust, where the How to be More Awesome journal was co-designed. Here are some personal stories from the canals to provide you with inspiration. Taken from the National Waterways archive, National Waterways Museum, Ellesmere Port.

'They'd teach you how to steer a boat for a start off, at an early age, and then they would set you off getting the locks ready for the boats to travel into, so they would gain time.' - Edward Ward remembering his childhood in Voices From the Waterways, by Jean Stone.

'It was a good form of transport. Cheap and safe. They reckon it saved a terrific amount of breakages because the journey was so smooth.' - Jim Morgan in Voices from the Waterways,
by Jean Stone.

'The wagons used to come up and tip the coal down a shoot and it used to go on the boats. Later it would be unloaded with a crane that grabbed it, but before that, there was a big bucket and we used to have to shovel it in.' - Leonard Waller in Voices from the Waterways, by Jean Stone

'I'm a harbour master and I've been working with waterways for about 30 years. When I started, about 1979, the canal was quite different then. We had the old diving system. It was what we called the Sieb-Gorman, where the diver got into one of these big brass helmets and the old canvas and leather suit and the big heavy boots and they had to trust the people upstairs. We had a big old wooden box that was trolleyed out to the lock side and you sat and wound the handle and that was the bellows that pumped the air down to the diver.' - Alex Hardy, harbour master, remembering his early working days (Courtesy of Dalriada Community History Project)

Be a poet

The Canal & River Trust has a Writer in Residence programme.
Have a look for it on the Trust website. Imagine the Canal &
River Trust has created a Young Poet in Residence scheme, and
to enter it you must provide a poem about the canals. Create
a poem and either have a poetry reading event in the school or
with your family.

Be an artist

Design a poster for the museum about water safety or a poster
to encourage the use of the waterways for leisure or education.
Then hold a school exhibition, or a competition. You'll need to
include the Canal & River Trust logo if you want to make it really
professional, which you can find online.

At its peak, the waterways
system covered 6,840 km
of navigable rivers and
canals and carried perhaps
30 million tons a year.

Reflections on the activities :

For all the activities provided in this part use the questions below to reflect and learn from the experience...

• What did you enjoy about the activity?

....

....

• If you did the activity again, what would you do differently?

....

....

• What did you learn from the experience?

....

....

Part 3.

Journaling

The River Severn is a famously tricky river. At certain times of the day it flows backwards.

This section uses your waterway experiences to help you be more positive about yourself. It also helps you to 'bounce back' when things are tough.

Scientific research shows that collecting good comments and thinking good thoughts for 28 days makes us happier.
Let's give it a try!

Day 1

Three good things...

Day 2

Three good things...

Day 3

Three good things...

Day 4

Three good things...

Did you know, cabins were decorated with hearts and clubs, but never spades, which bring bad luck

Day 5

Three good things...

Day 6

Three good things...

Day 7

Three good things...

Day 8

Three good things...

Day 9

Three good things...

Day 10

Three good things...

Day 11

Three good things...

Day 12

Three good things...

Day 13

Three good things...

Day 14

Three good things...

Did you know, Grand Union Canal is the longest canal in the UK? It goes from London to Birmingham and is 137 miles long.

The Seven Day Acts of Gratitude

Completing three acts of gratitude (helping someone, saying thanks or giving a compliment) helps your brain to work better and your wellbeing to improve. For the next seven days, think of someone you would like to thank. Then think about something you could do for them. It could be making them a card, sending a thank you message, making a small gift or just saying thank you.

Think about how these actions made you feel.

Note for teachers, group leaders and parents

To help young people get used to this activity, support them to start with small and simple observations, like a beautiful sky. You can also work in small groups and do the activity together, then compare ideas.

*Adapted from the Penn State University PRP (Penn Resilience Programme)

At the end of the 28 days, read through them all and choose the most important three. Take a few minutes to think, and write them down. As you read through them, notice how it makes you feel. Share your favourites with family or friends, or try it as part of a classroom activity.

If you're doing it at school, try sharing your comments on Post-it notes or as part of a drawing, and create a wall of positivity.

My act of gratitude...

Day 16

Three good things...

My act of gratitude...

Day 17

Three good things...

My act of gratitude...

Day 18

Three good things...

My act of gratitude...

Day 19

Three good things...

My act of gratitude...

Day 20

Three good things...

My act of gratitude...

The Seven Day Gratitude Challenge reflection

Now you've done the Seven Day Acts of Gratitude challenge, answer the questions below...

• What did you notice?

....

....

• How did other people react?

....

....

• What did you like about doing the activity?

....

....

Day 21

Three good things...

Day 22

Three good things...

Day 23

Three good things...

Day 24

Three good things...

Day 25

Three good things...

Day 26

Three good things...

Day 27

Three good things...

What were rams heads and swan necks used for on canal boats?

Day 28

Three good things...

Well done. You've achieved a lot!

Take time to think about your 28-day experience.

• What have you learned about yourself and others?
• What has surprised you?
• What have you enjoyed and found useful?
• What did you notice when you did the Seven Acts of Gratitude activity?
• What have been the best things about doing this book?
• What have you noticed about yourself and what are you doing differently? Ask someone you know what they have noticed...

Review and reflect

You've done really well. You've now completed the 28-day programme and the gratitude challenge, alongside lots of the other activities. Using the questions below, either get someone to interview you, or do it as a small group activity.

Don't forget to record your answers. You don't have to answer all of them at once, as you might need to do a bit of thinking, and you can always repeat it later.

What have been the best parts of visiting the waterways? Share your thoughts as a story.

- Which activities have you enjoyed most, and why?
- If this journal has been used as part of a museum visit, which parts excited and interested you the most?
- What did you like most about the waterways?
- What did you learn about yourself and other people?
- Having completed the 28-day 'three good things' exercise, did you notice anything different about yourself? (Helpful hint: ask your family or friends)
- What were your top three things in the 28 day journal?
- Which of your acts of gratitude had the biggest reaction, and why do you think that was?

If you'd like to share how much you have enjoyed and found this journal useful, send us an email at info@appreciatingpeople.co.uk, or tweet us on @AppreciatingP.

Part 4.

Extras

What can you do next?

If you've enjoyed this book and want to do some more journaling, explore your strengths and skills and try some fun learning activities, you'll like How to be More Awesome. How to be More Awesome is more than a journal – it's a structured resilience and confidence-building course that you can try individually, in groups or as a programme at school, or in your youth group.

It was co-designed with students from the Studio School, Northern Schools Trust, and includes a menu of exercises, some of which are similar to this journal. It also has jokes, unusual facts and inspirational quotes. Although we originally created it for 14 to 25 year olds, the oldest person using it is 70, and the youngest is three – with a bit of help from her dad. It's available to buy from the Appreciating People website – www.appreciatingpeople.co.uk – or from the National Waterways Museum shops.

This part is for teachers, education workers, parents and guardians, and provides guidance to help young people maximise what they get from the workbook. It includes helpful hints, information on the underlying methodology – like the importance of journaling, an explanation of Positive Psychology, Appreciative Inquiry, mindfulness, and wellbeing.

Helpful hints and guidance

- Activities and information about the museums and waterways are designed to enhance the museums experience and deepen knowledge;
- Many activities can be carried out either individually or in groups;
- Themes about fostering curiosity, encouraging learning, oral and written skills, reflecting on learning and having fun underpin all of the content;
- Elements highlighted in the 28 day journal will help flourishing, wellbeing and personal development, and foster resilience;
- Look at the TED talk by Shawn Achor on the Happiness Advantage (page 97) – it's a useful explanation of the importance of positive psychology and positive emotions. It's funny, too;
- Creative writing can be expanded into other activities such as poems, film and new articles
- Each activity has a set of reflective questions these can be completed either through in paired/group conversations or individually;
- Encourage people to explore and research the answers;
- Although primarily designed for eight to 13-year-olds, it's expected that people of all ages will be attracted to it;
- Many of the activities fit with national curriculum targets.

What is the 'cut'
in canal speak?

Useful websites

These are some useful pages to help you understand more about the work of the Canal & River Trust; how to get involved and be safe on our waterways, and an introduction to the amazing work the Trust does.

www.canalrivertrust.org.uk
www.canalrivertrust.org.uk/explorers

Health and wellbeing and the waterways

Our waterways are a great way to support and improve health and wellbeing in local communities. Research shows that health and wellbeing benefits can be derived from regular access to green (grassed, wooded or planted) and blue (water) environments. (1)

These benefits include increased levels of physical activity, which has an impact on obesity, strokes and cardiovascular disease. It also has benefits for some mental health conditions, by reducing stress and anxiety as a result of increased interaction with nature.

The quality of green and blue space is important in delivering good health benefits. They must be perceived as attractive, safe and accessible to attract those who may not currently exercise regularly in the open air.

Our waterways provide this sort of environment, and they're open to everyone. Although boats and boaters are very important to us, 95% of the users of our waterways are on dry land and catering for the needs of this group is an important part of our work. We provide a wide range of things beyond our activities to keep the canals and rivers operational, safe and attractive.

Across England and Wales we are exploring new ways to help ensure that our waterways meet the health and wellbeing needs of local communities. Many of our current activities already make a significant contribution to health and wellbeing, as part of the Five Ways to Wellbeing. Here are some examples...

 talk and listen,
be there,
feel connected

 do what you can,
enjoy what you do,
move your mood

 remember
the simple things
that give you joy

 embrace new experiences,
see opportunities,
surprise yourself

 your time,
your words,
your presence

We promote these to the public under the heading 'Waterways to Wellbeing' – you'll find out more on our website at: https://canalrivertrust.org.uk/news-and-views/features/waterways-to-wellbeing

Be active

With 2,000 traffic-free tow paths around the country you have the perfect excuse to get cycling, walking, running, canoeing and fishing! All great ways to boost endorphins and get you feeling fantastic.

Connect

Our waterways are full of friendly and enthusiastic people. You can easily get involved with the waterways community through the Canal & River Trust volunteering programme. There are hundreds of varied and flexible opportunities for you to explore. Why not give it a go and be part of a team making a real difference.

www.canalrivertrust.org.uk/volunteer

Take notice

Take time out to really look at the waterway environment. Take photographs, sketch, find a peaceful place to sit, have a picnic or try out the mindfulness exercise in this journal. Taking notice helps you to see new things, find new perspectives and improves your wellbeing.

Keep learning

Get involved with our learning team, take part in a visit, or volunteer with us! Visit our national waterways archive in Ellesmere Port. Come along to one of our open days, events or festivals. Drop in to one of our welcome stations. There's so much to learn and so many different ways to do it!

Give

We need your help to ensure that, in our increasingly fast-paced and crowded world, your canals and rivers remain vital local havens for people and nature. It could be the 200m stretch that you walk the dog along each morning, or that five mile towpath run you brave the cold for on a Sunday. We all have a story that connects us to the waterways. Why not join us as a friend of the Trust, supporting us and enjoying the benefits that brings.

www.canalrivertrust.org.uk/donate

Why journaling is important

You can adapt this information to form the content for a workshop and research project on journaling.

The word 'journaling' comes from the word 'journey'. Writing and using a journal is a personal thing, and should be seen as being a confidential process. Sharing information about the experience (rather than the content) is a great educational and learning opportunity.

Many of the exercises and tasks can be shared and used to chart people's progress. The important thing is that this needs be part of a personal decision and can be supported by an agreed contract with a friend/teacher/mentor.

Journaling is an ancient tradition. Throughout history, people have kept journals and diaries, contributing to our understanding of history. There's also increasing research to support the idea that journaling has a positive effect on personal wellbeing and provides a range of unexpected benefits.*

The act of writing accesses the left brain, which is analytical and rational. While your left brain is occupied, your right brain is free to create, be intuitive and feel. Recording things in your journal can help remove mental blocks. It allows you to use all of your brain power and strengths to better understand yourself, others and the world around you. Journaling has a number of benefits:

1. It helps you clarify your thoughts: taking a few moments to write down ideas can help you sort out the jumble of thoughts inside your brain.

2. It helps know yourself better: observing and writing regularly helps you get to know what makes you feel happy and confident, appreciate yourself, connect with your strengths, provide a clear view on situations and actions you're thinking of taking and people you may have to deal with, all of which are important for your emotional wellbeing.

3. Journaling helps to reduce stress; writing about things that

upset and challenge you helps to release these feelings, so you will feel calmer and better able to cope.

4. It helps solve problems more effectively: typically we solve problems via a left brain analytical perspective, but sometimes the problem can only be solved by engaging right-brained creativity and intuition. Writing and recording (including drawing and sketching) thoughts unlocks those abilities, providing the opportunity for unexpected solutions to arise.

5. It also helps resolve disagreements with others. Writing and recording about misunderstandings, concerns and issues can avoid stewing about the matter. It will help you understand different views and contribute to a resolution.

6. Journaling allows you to track patterns, trends, improvements, and personal development over a period of time.

* Purcell, M. (2006): The Health Benefits of Journaling in Psych Central. Retrieved on June 25, 2014, from bit.ly/NO_jour.

Appreciative journaling adds another dimension to journaling. It's about actively seeking the good side of a situation and seeing how we can expand on that. We're not asking you to ignore or whitewash difficult situations or experiences, but rather than 'ruminating' and wasting energy on things which increase your negative emotions, search out and focus on positive ones.

What we put our attention on grows in our minds

Ruminating is the name we give to focusing on negative thoughts. It's like a record that's stuck and keeps repeating the same lines. For example, replaying an argument with a friend in your head. Research has shown that rumination is associated with a variety of negative consequences; appreciative journaling is a very helpful alternative.

Training started young! At the age of three, children would learn how to steer a narrow boat, standing on a stool.

Positive psychology

Positive psychology is the scientific study of positive aspects of human life, such as happiness, wellbeing and flourishing. It looks at how these qualities develop and grow and how can we maintain them.

Professor Martin Seligman is the founding father of positive psychology and a major figure in the wellbeing movement. He believes that a happier society requires us to pay more attention to the quality of our inner life, and to use proven methods to improve it. That is what positive psychology is about; it goes beyond the treatment of depression and anxiety to ways we could all lead more rewarding lives.

The exercises and approach it offers include the systematic practice of kindness, gratitude to others, counting your blessings and exploiting your strengths rather than attacking your weaknesses. It also teaches resilience and optimism. Positive psychology is one of the newest branches of psychology. The first World Congress of Positive Psychology was held in 2009.

Some positive psychology research findings:

• People are generally happy;
• Money does not necessarily buy wellbeing: but spending money on other people does;
• Some of the best ways to combat disappointments and setbacks include social relationships and character strengths;
• Work can be important to wellbeing, especially when people are able to engage in work that is purposeful and meaningful;
• While happiness is influenced by genetics, people can learn to be happier by developing optimism, gratitude and altruism.

Have you ever wondered why the world seems more inclusive and open when you're in a good mood, and why your circumstances seem so narrow when you're feeling down? How can you nurture the good feelings so they last longer and have more powerful effects on your life? Dr Barbara Fredrickson is an author (Positivity and Love 2.0) and leading scholar in the area of positive psychology.

Her 'broaden-and-build' theory explains why positive emotions change your perspective on life and how they can help you develop valuable emotional resources, like resilience and mindfulness. She has found, in over 20 years of research, that individuals need to keep a certain ratio of positive emotions to negative ones in order to flourish. The video Positive Emotions Open Our Mind highlights her work — you can watch it on YouTube: bit.ly/NO_PP.

Three particularly notable things about positive emotions are:

• They help us be more open. For example, a number of experiments have been done where giving students a gift of sweets before an exam helps them feel more positive before they start and they then do better in the exam
• They help people find better 'win-win' solutions

• They help people be more resilient

It's interesting to note over 60 UK schools are now using positive psychology approaches (Google Action for Happiness). Martin Seligman and his colleagues at Penn State University have developed a range of wellbeing programmes for schools, the military and hospitals.

Mindfulness

Have you ever opened a bag of crisps or a bar of chocolate, and found that you've eaten it all in a flash, without really noticing? That you've done something on autopilot, and don't even remember it? More people are beginning to understand that having our 'minds full' of things to do or worry about is not good for us. Being 'mindful' is about taking notice of what we're doing. Being 'in the moment', even just for two minutes at a time, helps our mind and bodies to relax.

Jon Kabat-Zinn is a famous teacher of mindfulness meditation. His definition of mindfulness is: 'Mindfulness means paying attention in a particular way; On purpose, in the present moment, and non-judgmentally.'

The ABC of mindfulness

A is for awareness: Becoming more aware of what you're thinking and doing; of what's going on in your mind and body

B is for 'just being' with your experience: Avoiding the tendency to respond on autopilot and feed problems by creating your own story

C is for seeing things and responding more wisely. By creating a gap between the experience and our reaction to it, we can make wiser choices.

This mnemonic (a system of letters or associations for remembering information) was created by Juliet Adams. You'll find more at: bit.ly/NO_MF.

Appreciative Inquiry

Central to this journal is the organisational and community development process called Appreciative Inquiry (AI). The term 'appreciative' comes from the idea that when something increases in value it 'appreciates'. 'Inquiry' describes the process of seeking to understand through questions, and the value of paying attention to the things that, if increased, add value and make a difference.

What
are Tom
puddings
and
where
will you
find
them?

Did you know,
a cow fell in the
canal near Foulridge
Tunnel on the Leeds &
Liverpool Canal and swam all
the way through before getting out!

AI is the cousin of positive psychology and part of the growing movement to focus on and build from the strengths and assets of people and groups. By working from this positive focus (as opposed to focusing on what's not working) people become more resilient and creative. They develop and deliver success and achieve realistic solutions to problems.

First developed by David Cooperrider in the late 1980s at Case Western University in the USA, it's now used all over the world by large and small organisations, communities, schools and in personal development programmes. At the heart of the approach are questions and conversations that are interesting, informative and help you learn about yourself and the people and groups around you.

A useful definition from David Cooperrider: 'AI is a process for engaging people in building the kinds of organisations and a world they want to live in. Working from people's strengths and positive experiences, AI co-creates a future based on collaboration and dialogue.'

It's important to remember that AI is not about positive thinking, but about how we create change, individually and collectively. It's not about ignoring problems, but looking at them differently.

More information about Appreciative Inquiry and its application can be found on www.appreciatingpeople.co.uk and www.bemoreawesome.net.

Alongside a model for organisational and community development, AI has contributed to different approaches in mentoring, coaching, forward-planning, leadership, team building, counselling and international development. It is the key underpinning methodology to all Appreciating People's journals.

Appreciative living

Appreciative living is an easy to understand, practical approach to help you focus on what's good and get clear about what you want. It draws on the principles of AI and works for individuals, families and groups.

The National Joy Study that Appreciative Living founder, Jackie

Kelm, carried out in 2007 showed that just three fast and easy Appreciative Living exercises led 97% of participants to feel significantly happier in just 28 days... and they continued to feel that way six months later.

There are three basic steps in Appreciative Living:

1. Appreciating the present
2. Imagining the ideal
3. Acting in alignment (actions and thoughts being aligned with what you want)

The importance of gratitude & the 'happiness advantage'

We tend to think 'I'll be happy when I pass my exams,' or 'I'll be happy when I have enough friends.' Whenever we reach a goal our happiness level doesn't really rise — we just set ourselves another goal we have to reach. Shawn Achor writes very clearly about the need to turn our way of thinking on its head — be happy first, and let success follow.

If we can be happy in the moment (rather than deferring it until we are 'successful') then the brain experiences a happiness advantage. Your brain performs better — intelligence rises, your creativity and energy rises. The brain is 31% more effective — 37% better at sales; doctors are 19% better at correct diagnoses; dopamine makes you happier and turns on all the learning centres in your brain. In just two minutes a day for 21 days in a row, your brain can be rewired to work more optimistically and more successfully — just by writing down three new things each day that you appreciate.

Journaling about one positive experience over the past 24 hours allows your brain to relive it and you receive the benefits. Exercise teaches your brain that your behaviour matters. Meditation and mindfulness help us undo the stress of multi-tasking. Send one text or Facebook message to a friend saying something you appreciate about them or a strength of theirs that you like – create ripples of positivity.

(Research taken from The Happiness Advantage: The seven principles of positive psychology that fuel success and performance at work and The happy secret to better work a TED talk by Shawn Achor: bit.ly/NO_SA.)

Additional support

We'll be using social media as a way of collecting your ideas, thoughts and work… If you're interested in learning more about appreciative living, appreciative inquiry and positive psychology, we recommend you visit www.appreciativeliving.com and our site at www.appreciatingpeople.co.uk.

Final advice – keep journaling

You can do this by getting a notebook and adapting the questions used in this book, or buy How to be More Awesome if you want some structure.

Birmingham Canal system has more canals than Venice. The Birmingham Canal Network (BCN) covers over 100 miles of canals.

Part 5.

More info

We've drawn a lot from the work of the pioneers of positive psychology and the freely available material on the web which has allowed it to spread and grow – thank you to everyone who has contributed to that work. Much appreciation is also due to the generous and inspired AI practitioners worldwide whose work has guided and influenced us. A special mention goes to Jackie Kelm, Appreciative Living, who inspired Appreciating People to develop the appreciative journaling programme.

Number One would not have happened without the support and encouragement of a number of people. Including Lucy Bowles-Lewis, Canal & River Trust; Graham Boxer, Canal & River Trust; Rachel Dove, English lead at The Studio, Liverpool/Northern Schools Trust; Lorna Kernahan, Greenfield Valley Heritage Park; National Waterways Museum young curators; Samantha Marine, Canal & River Trust; Rhiannon Moore; Suzanne Quinney, AI adviser and the Wordscapes team.

Authors

This resource was created by Tim Slack, co-director, Appreciating People and Helen Evans, education coordinator, Canal & River Trust museums.

Appreciating People works with people, communities, business, charities and organisations and social enterprises to help them get the best out of themselves. We work regionally, nationally and internationally from our base in Liverpool, UK. Appreciative Inquiry is at the heart of everything we do, supporting organisational development, resilience, adaptability, innovation and wellbeing across local authorities, private businesses, communities, hospitals, universities and social enterprises. Tim Slack is a co-founder of Appreciating People.

http://www.appreciatingpeople.co.uk/

Wordscapes

Wordscapes is an award-winning non-fiction publisher and storyteller. Based in Liverpool, we work with clients locally, nationally and internationally, publishing a range of books, magazines, newspapers and films to help them communicate their stories. Have a look at www.wordscape.org.uk.

Illustrator – Sian McArthur

Sian is an artist and illustrator living in Liverpool. With a back-ground in fine art and sculpture, she creates art with a purpose as part of the 'More Than Minutes' team, providing visual records of events and conferences as 'visual minutes'. She is passionate about drawing and illustration, as well as making things.

If you'd like to get in touch with Sian regarding illustration or visual minutes, contact Appreciating People (tim@appreciatingpeople. co.uk) for further details.

• Days out and special events: https://canalrivertrust.org.uk/

Did you know, Fossdyke Canal is the oldest canal in Britain and was built by the Romans

Notes

Notes

Notes

Notes

Notes

Notes

Notes

Notes

Notes

Notes

Notes

Number One –
An Activity Book + Journal

Written by Helen Evans and Tim Slack
Design and production: Louis Tuckman
Illustrations: Sian McArthur
Editor: Fiona Shaw
Editorial assistant: Jack Atkins
Proofreading by Lucy Chesters and Gill Harrison

Printed and bound in the UK by Resolution Print Management

ISBN: 978-0-9955594-7-9

First published in November 2017 by:

Wordscapes Ltd.
The Mezzanine,
Northern Lights Building,
5 Mann Street
Liverpool L8 5AF

www.wordscape.org.uk

Along the waterways there are: 1,000 wildlife conservation sites, 650km of conservation area, 2,756 listed buildings, 51 scheduled monuments, 5 World Heritage Sites, 1,654 locks, 54 tunnels, 3,115 bridges, 417 aqueducts, 91 reservoirs, 965 km of hedgerow. Enjoy them!